FOCUS

The simple power of being
focused in our work

Jack Ricchiuto

DesigningLife Books

Books by Jack Ricchiuto

Collaborative Creativity / 1996

Accidental Conversations / 2002

Project Zen / 2003

Appreciative Leadership / 2005

Mountain Paths / 2007

Conscious Becoming / 2008

Instructions From The Cook / 2009

The Stories That Connect Us / 2010

The Enchantment Of Casual Origins / 2011

The Joy Of Thriving / 2012

Ordinary Eyes / 2012

The Agile Planning Field Guide / 2012

Abundant Possibilities / 2013

The Power Of Circles / 2013

Making Sense Of Time / 2014

Beyond Recipes / 2014

Focus / 2015

Focus | 3

Focus

Published by DesigningLife Books

1020 Kenilworth Avenue

Cleveland OH 44113 USA

FocusAtWork.info

ISBN 978-1508937555

Paperback

1. Work. Professional Development. Personal Growth.
Organization. Leadership.
I. Title

Printed in the USA

Production: CreateSpace

Cover Art: Tia Andrako

Content

The nature of focus

The practice of focus

Deepening focus

Focus at work

Invitation

No era in human history has seen the kinds of change, complexity and connectivity at work we are seeing now. In this landscape, the most vital competency is our capacity for focus.

When we are focused, we work with a sense of clarity and calmness. We are less distracted and reactive. We get more done. We see possibilities we would otherwise miss. We enjoy more of what life offers us to enjoy. In our work, focus is the dog that wags the tail of everything good.

Clarity and calmness are optimal spaces for engaging our strengths and passions. Working from our strengths and passions makes our weaknesses and self-doubts less relevant. Focus keeps us creative, connected and agile.

In this exploration of focus, I draw wisdom from the neurosciences and over three decades of research and work in positive psychology and work with thousands of groups in over two dozen industries and sectors.

Our best intentions have power when we show up with focus. Focus is the power of surfing the waves of change that contour our landscapes of work. When we see things in our work going well, it's because we are focused.

Focus is a consciousness that creates the energy vibrations of a clear, calm mind. The quality of our attention is the most significant factor in the narratives of our success. This is the simple power of focus.

Jack Ricchiuto
March 2015

The Nature Of Focus

The primacy of focus

Focus is the mother of all things good. It is the source of our best moments in our work.

When we are focused in our work, we do our best. When focus follows us home, our work enriches rather than compromises the quality of our life.

We attribute our best ideas, connections and accomplishments to focus. When we're focused we pay attention to details and the quality of our work reflects that. We follow through on things and the currency of our trustworthiness buys us a lot of influence real estate. When our work is alive with daily juggling done well, we keep an amazing number of objects in flow.

Focus isn't a choice. It's thousands of choices. It's a habit.

We are focused in our work precisely to the extent we daily practice it. We don't have to learn focus because it's hardwired into our brains. We can learn how to intentionally practice and develop it more.

Focus

Working with focus is working with a clear, calm mind.

We all have moments of being naturally focused in our work. Our intentions are clear. We get one thing done after another. We aren't distracted by things we can't control. We aren't reactive to things we don't plan. We know what we intend and we realize it.

Some of us have more moments of focus than others. As we're now seeing in the neurosciences research, our ability to be focused is a matter of practice. The core difference between people who have more or fewer moments of focus in their work is how much time they spend working with focus.

When we are focused, it's because we create it. The more we realize how we create our own moments of focus, the more possible focus becomes.

The neurosciences are now unraveling the secrets to what happens in the clear and calm moments of focus.

Brain imaging indicates that our mind is optimally clear when we experience any kind of curiosity. Our mind is optimally calm when we experience any kind of rhythms. A clear, calm mind is a focused mind alive with the light energy vibrations of curiosity and rhythm.

From her background in the neurosciences, Tamsin Astor talks about how one of the most fundamental and powerful rhythms in life are the rhythms of change in time.

Life is change. Change happens in the micro rhythms of moments and days and the macro rhythms of weeks and months. Each one is different from the last. No two pulses in time are exactly alike.

When we are focused, we are curious about how change happens in each rhythm of time. We compare the subtle and significant differences between this conversation and the last, between our sense of our world now and a moment or any timeframe ago.

This amazing synergy between curiosity and rhythm opens the space of focus, the space making it possible to be at our best.

When we're unfocused, our attention to change is passive and fragmented. We don't notice change from a space of curiosity. We don't notice change in time rhythm comparisons between moments and days, weeks and months. A passive and fragmented view of change is all it takes to be distracted and reactive.

A distracted and reactive mind uses more energy than it creates. It is an unsustainable way of working that leads to a life of postponements, missed opportunities and excuses.

When we return to curiosity about the rhythms of change, we return to focus. It's that simple and powerful. When we create focus, our work is abundant with energy, passion and connection. We flow easily in the direction of our intentions.

In sync with change

The more we remain curious about how things change in the rhythms of time, the clearer and calmer our mind becomes. With a clear mind, we become more able to see new possibilities. With a calm mind, we become more able to easily act on them.

Just noticing change in the micro and macro rhythms of life has this power.

When physicists uncover the essence of matter, they find change. Change is life's constant and character.

When we have eyes for it, it becomes obvious that change is happening throughout and beyond our organizations and work groups.

Our sense of things changes from one day and week to the next. Our intentions and questions continuously evolve as the world around us shifts and changes in expected and unpredictable ways.

What people expect from us and how they experience what we deliver shifts for them over time. What we have available changes. What we enjoy about each other and our work shifts. Only in the delusion of continuity does it seem we work in a world that isn't changing.

We are optimally focused when we are curious about the sea of change on which we surf.

Focus is not obsession with continuities. It is being in sync with change. The more in sync with change we become, the more naturally focused we are.

Information overload

There is an interesting relationship between the quantity of information we daily consume and the quality of our focus.

With the endless proliferation of digital content producers, now magnified by crowdsourcing, there is a spiraling galaxy of shiny objects of attention that can keep us regularly distracted and reactive, and not in good ways. Content deprivation doesn't help.

Focus is not necessarily related to hedonistic information indulgence nor heroic data dieting.

Our prefrontal cortex manages our ability to focus. Stanford research demonstrates our brain goes into distraction and reaction mode when the information we consume, even by a small margin, exceeds the capacity of our prefrontal cortex.

We lose focus and when we lose focus we lose will power. Will power has no power when we lack focus, even when our intentions are sincere and compelling.

When we are in prefrontal cortex overload, we can even question our commitment to our intentions because we fail to follow through on them.

The good news is that the practice of focus builds our prefrontal cortex capacity and our ability to realize our intentions in any contours of information landscapes.

When we're overloaded with data, information and the noise of opinions, we can try to concentrate.

In concentration, we narrow our attention to block out the noise of shiny objects in our experience. We work overtime resisting distractions and reactions that get in the way of seeing something through.

Concentration takes great effort because it adds an extra layer of tension from continuously fighting shiny objects. This tension makes concentration effective at a cost.

The difference between concentration and focus is that in focus, we don't need extra energy to narrow down our attention by continuously warding off pesky attention pirates.

In focus, we simply work with intention and curiosity about what's different from one moment and day to the next. This creates the kind of clarity and calmness that allows us to get things done and enjoyed.

Change blindness

Psychologist Melissa Beck, PhD, of George Mason University has studied change blindness. This is our inability to notice visual changes in our world.

She points out that two kinds of change occur in our experience: changes we consider probable and improbable. The research indicates that we are twice as likely to not notice improbable changes in our world than we do probable changes.

Until we develop our capacity for focus, we miss all kinds of changes literally in front of us. We don't notice new ideas and possibilities. We don't notice how opportunity doors have closed or opened.

Further research shows that when people work together closely in groups, their tendency toward change blindness decreases. They notice more change and just being more aware of change makes them measurably smarter and faster together.

High performing groups stay in sync with change. They talk about how things are shifting and changing. It's precisely their attention to change that makes it easy for them to stay focused no matter how information and ambiguity rich their work landscapes become.

Follow through

When we are focused, we follow through. We complete things we start. When we are distracted and reactive, things go undone. Each undone thing becomes another shiny object in our consciousness decreasing our ability to focus.

Every time we have ever followed through with an intention, it was because we were focused in clear intentions.

The more why, how and when details we have for any intention, the more clear it is. Intentions lacking these details languish. Even with passion or urgency, unclear intentions do not easily move into action and fulfillment

Being focused creates space for clarity. The more focused we are, the clearer our intentions. The more intentions we follow through on, the more energy we have for focus in our work. It's a virtuous energy spiral.

The business case

The more focused we become, the more everything about our organization makes sense. We unveil the mysteries of performance and outcomes. Our understanding emerges from one simple, powerful realization: *Everyone does the best they can given the quality of their attention at the time.*

Not sometimes. Always. Attention is that significant. It is more significant than anything else. When we get attention right, everything goes right.

We can engineer all kinds of strategies and structures, programs and policies, accountabilities and incentives. If people aren't focused, none of these matter. They only matter when people are focused.

Lack of focus is the mother of a million things mistaken and neglected. We miss details and deadlines. We miss subtle cues to new possibilities in conversations. We leave important resources less than fully engaged. We leave money on the table and inspiration at the door. Things take far longer than they need.

Doing better and helping others do better is a matter of expanding the scope of their everyday attention. It is being focused. It is noticing change.

We can trace every good thing that happens in and for organizations back to some specific moments of people being focused in clarity and calmness rather than unfocused in distraction and reaction.

The costs of being distracted and reactive are many. When we are unfocused, we pay more attention to what we don't have, can't do and aren't getting done than what we do have, can do and are getting done.

We miss deadlines. We overpromise and underdeliver, disappointing even our own standards and principles. We make things more complicated and arduous than they need be.

We resist change and as a result miss opportunities. We become limited by our own self-fulfilling expectations. We have to sustain an affordable level of noise and drama to distract us from the inconsolable restlessness of persistent distraction and reaction. We feel unengaged, uninspired and tired.

Each of these come about simply because we live and work without focus, because we don't pay attention to how things change in ourselves, our life and our world.

As easy as it is to criticize others for lack of sensitivity, motivation or contribution, these are all symptoms of working without focus. Focus brings out the best in everyone because it puts us in sync with the constant of change.

Focus is core to working with a positive attitude. Gallup's engagement research indicates that the core difference between lower and higher performing individuals, teams and leaders is perspective.

Clarity and calmness

Our moments of clarity are moments of knowing the optimal timing of what could and should be done. Timing is everything. We know what we want to do, what we could do, what we should do. We are more clear on the best timing of these when we pay attention to change. Knowing the best timing makes the difference between doing well and struggling to do well.

When we work with clarity we're not distracted. We know the difference between what we know and assume. We know the difference between shiny objects and important opportunities for agility. We are present, undistracted by noise.

Our moments of calmness are moments of feeling centered. Our sense of calmness gives us a certain buoyancy in whatever conditions and circumstances we're in as our energy vibrations of focus are light.

When we are in sync with change, we are in sync with all that is. In that possibility space is a durable serenity that keeps us more responsive than reactive.

When we work with calmness, we don't work from reflexive habits. We work from reflective responsiveness to the subtle and significant changes emerging and shifting from one moment and day to the next. We create the light energy vibrations that makes for a clear and calm mind in whatever we do.

Static

It's fascinating and significant that static connotes signal distorting noise, lack of change and a cause of clinging. It is the quintessential character of being unfocused.

Being unfocused creates the static of distraction and reaction. It makes listening difficult and less likely. It gets in the way of our ability to empathize, be present, show up, notice new connections, make new connections, follow through and act with agility and responsiveness.

We are unfocused precisely when we have a static view of ourselves and our world. We allow our attention to be more dominated by seeming continuities than by the ubiquity of change.

Intuition

Clarity and calmness of focus creates ideal conditions for intuition. When we don't have enough data to act and action is necessary now, intuition skillfully guides us in the direction of our success.

Many of the important changes in our experience and world that represent new possibilities emerge in subtle forms. Anyone unfocused would not notice them even though they are hidden in plain sight.

People who have developed their intuition pick up subtle clues and gain an immediate and palpable *sense* of new possibilities emerging.

The value of intuition is how it informs curiosity. We ask and pursue questions when we have a *feeling* about something. Intuition is a way of knowing we experience but can't explain. It deepens and expands curiosity.

We can build intuition simply by paying attention to and testing our shifting sensations, feelings and emotions in various situations. Testing means more observing, inquiry and exploration into what is actually emerging.

We get better with practice. The more focused we become, the more strongly intuitive we become.

Focus is simple

Focus is ridiculously simple. We notice change. That's all there is to it. If you're looking for complicated, being unfocused will soothe your mistrust of simple.
We all have the ability to make things more difficult than they need to be. We make complicated what could otherwise be simple. It is precisely our being unfocused that makes this possible.

We don't have to learn how to focus. It's hard wired into our brains. We don't have to go through training or classes. We don't need advanced certifications or degrees. We don't have to wedge it into our learning goals and performance review commitments.

Nor do we need to trek up ancient mountains to sit at the feet of gurus. We don't need any special equipment or apps. We don't have to become better people. We already know how to pay attention to change. It's what our mind know how to do naturally.

We don't need any special conditions. We don't need bosses or peers with unconditional love. We don't need managerial bribes or incentives. We don't have to keep up with the latest fashion in management fads. We don't need to drink from the firehoses of motivational speakers or follow all the cool people on social media.

We can be focused anywhere, anytime. We can be focused locally and virtually, in meetings and in the solitude of our todo lists. We can be focused with full and empty inboxes, with whatever personalities show up at the table of collaborations.

We can focus in the midst of emotional fire storms and quiet lulls in any day, week or project. We can focus when things are messy and orderly, in a state of chaos and simplicity. Focus makes our sense of attention flawless.

All we do is notice what's new in each rhythm of time. It's just that simple.

Wiring our brain for focus

The neurosciences demonstrate there are no permanent structures in the brain. When people learn and practice focus, even after a few weeks, we see changes in the structures of their brain. This ability of the mind to change the structure of the brain simply by paying attention differently is neuroplasticity.

The good news is that we can build our capacity for focus by practicing attention to how things change in each moment and day. Our experiences of clarity and calmness are vibrational energy signals of how our brain builds greater capacity for working with focus.

It doesn't matter how distracted and reactive we are. It doesn't matter how much technology we have or wear. It doesn't matter how much or little we take on in our work and life. It doesn't matter if we're hipsters or boomers.

The neuroplasticity of our brain is not a function of early cognitive development. It's the design of our brain for the duration of our life.

At any point in time, we can practice our way into a new brain. If we equate brain patterns to personality, then we get to discover ways to expand the footprint of our personality into new ways of thinking and being in our world. History is not destiny. We are stuck only with what we believe we are stuck with.

The more time we spend being focused, the more focused we become. The more it becomes second nature. We never forget how to be distracted and reactive. The ability to be unfocused simply becomes less relevant. Our strengths and passions become more available and our happiness set points improve.

We remain present to change and in this presence show up with our best.

The Practice Of Focus

5 Practices of focus

There are infinite ways to practice focus. Here is a handful of approaches we can seamlessly weave into our everyday work.

Moments: Notice how each moment is different

Our experience of life is fluid, continuously in flux. There is something about each new moment that is different from the last. It can be a certain feeling or sound, thought or observation. The differences can be significant and subtle.

When we show up in a conversation with focus, we notice shifts in the unfolding and ever-shifting tones and expressions of people's faces, voices and gestures. We notice shifts in our own. We notice how different memories and associations come and go like clouds, unless we get distracted by them.

Our moment to moment experience shifts even in the simple habits of returning messages or emails, taking a walk, eating a snack or meal, sipping on the beverage of the hour. To notice these shifts is being focused.

Even when we're sitting with a question or decision, focus means paying attention to how our experience unfolds in the declaration of our questions and decisions. We notice how each moment is different. We notice how new possibilities emerge because focus opens the space of clarity and calmness.

Inquiries: Go into anything with new questions to discover new things about our world

The more we notice how no two consecutive moments are exactly the same, it becomes obvious that the future is intrinsically unknowable. We discover that even the exact character of the next moment is not knowable when we are in this moment before.

When we are focused, we greet the world with boundless curiosity.

The world is not intrinsically interesting or uninteresting. It is as interesting as we have curiosity for it. Our world stays vibrantly interesting when we create and realize new questions about it. It's good practice to always have far more questions that we could ever have the time or resources to answer. Just having an interesting world and the ability to make life a continuous journey of learning is enough for focus.

With focus, we engage in our world with new questions. We read and observe with new questions. We take on each new change with new questions. We go into every planned and unplanned conversation with new questions. We listen with curiosity. When life becomes more interesting, we notice more details and patterns. We act with wisdom.

More questions lead to better questions. Better questions lead to better discoveries and decisions.

Uniqueness: Notice things that don't fit the norm

With focus, we notice things at the edges, the outliers, the different from the generalized norms. We notice the value of the unique.

We appreciate how things grow into uniqueness. We notice this with the groups we work with. We notice this with our organization's brand and strategies. We notice the unique strengths and passions we bring to any conversation, decision, task and project.

We now have evidence that over the centuries and eras, human beings have become increasingly more civilized, less violent and oppressive. As we live longer, we become more inventive about how to create quality lives worthy of longer lives.

Interesting that in the last hundred years there were unique people whose inner voices called them to do what was normatively considered technically, socially, financially and politically impossible. They uniquely envisioned things that would impossibly eliminate diseases, close economic gaps, democratize education, empower women and connect a planet as never before.

We live with simple focus every time we notice how we and anyone in our world are in any way unique. We celebrate the beauty and power of difference.

Expectations: Expect that what we experience will be somehow different, new, changed

It's easy to notice the persistent relationship between expectation and experience. We experience what we expect to experience. We expect something will be a good or bad time, and it turns out to be.

When we expect things to be the same, that's what we notice. This is how we can stay unfocused in our work week after week and year after year. Each of us is capable of spending whole careers busily unfocused.

Expecting differences is based in the simple acknowledgment that the world outside our awareness changes in more ways than we can and will ever know.

This is the powerful realization that we see what we look for. It's the practice of looking differently. The world looks different when we look differently.

Shifts: Notice what's shifting for you in the contexts of what you know, feel, believe

Being human is a symbiosis between how we shape our world and how it shapes us. We are changed in the act of changing our world.

Something is always shifting for us. How we understand ourselves, each other, the drama of our world shifts. How we feel about each other shifts. What we know about new opportunities and commitments shifts. How we feel about how we're doing and what we're dreaming shifts.

Some shifts are subtle, others are more significant. We notice them and they become intuitive guides to noticing and engaging new possibilities on the edges of familiarities.

Every crossroads represents a shift of some kind. Crossroads in a project or career are prime opportunities to be focused.

Context and content

Our everyday experience has two dimensions, context and content. Context is how things change. Content is what changes.

Content is our experience of sense and sense making events. Sense events include anything we see, hear, feel, smell and taste. Sense making events include anything we remember, imagine, question, declare and narrate. When we notice the context of our experience, we naturally also notice its content.

Noticing change happens more easily when we pay attention primarily to the context of our experience, how things change. When we get caught up in thinking and talking about content, it becomes easy to miss how things are changing.

Attention to content fosters awareness of continuities to the exclusion of changes. When we focus, we focus on context.

Generalizations and opinions

We are prone to be unfocused when we encounter intolerable amounts of uncertainty and ambiguity.

Being unfocused creates a sense of continuity because we're giving attention to what we think isn't changing.

We give less attention to what's new and changing because it represents the root of intolerable uncertainty and ambiguity. A sense of continuity comforts us and anesthetizes the tension of the unknown.

The language of generalization fuels the persistent sticky quality of being unfocused. The language of generalization is *all, none, always, never* and the *norm*. When we don't greet uncertainty and ambiguity with focus, lack of focus runs on generalizations. Stress and boredom are the children of generalizations. They are possible with being unfocused.

With focus, we live in harmony with the reality of change. We expect things to be different with our customers and clients, vendors and partners. We expect things to change with our groups and leaders. We expect things to shift in how we define and time our commitments. We trust no generalization.

We are born into rich ecologies of opinions. Opinions include any kinds of assessments and assumptions. As we expand our life footprint, some are elevated to the status of immutable useful truths. Others are dismissed as outdated, not so useful truths.

When we are unfocused in distraction and reaction, we have great faith in our opinions. They can feel like important data points, especially if we convert others to our assumptions.

Even our more cherished opinions can have little to do with how our experience and world is changing. They can diminish focus, leading down roads to nowhere rewarding or even interesting. The less focused we are, the more time we spend trading and wrestling in opinions.

Opinions get sticky when we continue to practice them to the exclusion of curiosity. We create strong brain connections between specific kinds of events and specific kinds of opinions. When we greet opinions, ours or those of others, with focus, we weaken these connections.

Opinions become less and less sticky with the practice of focus. We liberate ourselves into spaces of new perspectives and possibilities.

Generalizations and opinions are the proud parents of reactions. The more we become unfocused with even the most sincere generalizations and opinions, the more reactive we are to what happens, and doesn't happen, in our life and world.

Being reactive is contagious. Our reactivity sparks and sustains the same in others. As we become less reactive, the same becomes more possible for them. We are better together when we are less reactive together. When we intend to make it easier for others to be and do their best, we are most helpful when we are not reactive.

The power of intention

Intentions are declarations of what we would love to be possible.

Given that the future is intrinsically unknowable, we consider intentions flexible lenses revealing present opportunities rather than fixed locations indicating predictable accomplishments.

The neurosciences indicate that there is a close positive relationship between how we experience present opportunities and future intentions. The depth and clarity of our passion in the present is equal to the breadth and depth of our intentions into the future.

In this context, we can have as many detailed intentions going out as far into the future as we want. They can be personal or global, realistic or impossible. We don't have to defend them nor jealously protect them from change. They are lenses into an intrinsically unknowable future revealing new opportunities in an actionable present. When we work with focus, we work with continuously emerging and evolving intentions.

Subtle practice

In our moment to moment experience, we come across things that are persistently sticky. They grab our attention in ways that make us distracted and reactive.

They're bothersome memories of past conversations, emails or texts. They're annoying questions that get us up in the morning or keep us up at night. They're negative feelings that just won't go away. They're energy draining sensations like headaches, not feeling well, strong emotions, stress or fatigue. They are unfinished tasks, uncertain outcomes, unclear expectations, undelivered promises, unwelcome issues, unresolved decisions.

The more we try to distract ourselves from them and react to them, the more persistent they become. What we resist persists.

Focus means choosing a persistent object of attention and holding it in the space of our attention. Then we simply notice how our experience in that space naturally shifts and changes from one moment to the next. We notice how each next moment of attention differs from the one before.

As we infuse the dense energy of sticky objects with the light energy of focus, the dense energy dissipates and shifts into a palatable lightness.

In focus, we feel like a spacious sky letting any kinds of weather in flux and things in flight come and go. We realize our clear and calm nature. We see suffering soften, obsessions diminish and cravings lose their hold on us. If and as they reemerge, we greet them again with the subtle practice of simple focus.

In her Harvard research, Ellen Langer sees people actually begin to enjoy doing tasks they used to hate simply by bringing a sense of focus to those tasks. Focus has this transformational power.

The transition from unfocused to focused

As we move toward becoming more focused, we don't make being unfocused a problem. When we're unfocused it's simply because we're so good at. Being unfocused is an opportunity for understanding rather than criticism. All that matters is returning back to focus wherever we are. We work with simple questions. Here are some samples.

- What am I noticing in my world now that I wasn't paying attention to yesterday?

- What's new in my world this week compared to last week?
- Is my sense of success and progress shifting or changing in any ways?
- What trends am I noticing in what I'm tracking through all the various media I'm using to keep up with my world the the larger world?
- When it comes to what they are paying attention to, what seems to be different about people I'm working with today and this week compared to yesterday and last week?
- How has the last couple hours been different from the couple before that?
- What's different about this conversation compared to the last we had?
- What's different in this moment right now compared to the moment before?

It helps to be inventive with other kinds of questions that can spark focus. In the process we discover the deep, intrinsic and enduring relationship between focus and curiosity.

Breaths of focus

One of the easiest ways to build our brain's capacity for focus is in relatively quiet spaces. It could be sitting comfortably somewhere, on a walk or doing a routine task that takes little complex attention.

We work with the natural rhythm of our breath to mark each moment of noticing what's different in our experience of each fresh moment.

We allow the breath to shift and flow naturally without making any attempt to alter or control its flow. We count our breaths from one to ten. We can count on each full breath or on each inhale and exhale.

On each count, we simply notice anything different about that moment compared to the last. When we lose count or get lost in some content, we just return to one. This is a simple practice we can do often that allows the mind to settle into the flow of focus.

We can do this for a couple minutes and increase the duration when we have the time and as we become more familiar with it. The more we do it, the easier it gets and the deeper our focus becomes.

Any intention we set at the end of this kind practice has a good chance of being realized because we are most able to realize our intentions when we are focused.

But my body is amazing

An energetic genre of people embark on the journey toward greater focus because they thought an amazing body would automatically create focus. They have evidence it doesn't.

Building focus requires specific mind practice. Doing yoga and working out in a gym, even going to intensive classes, builds stronger bodies but not necessarily stronger minds unless the mind practice of focus is explicitly included.

Being good at focus is a habit of mind that needs to be intentionally and specifically built. Building strong mind character takes as much rigor as building strong body character. So every physical discipline supports the discipline of growing capacity for focus.

Being fit and healthy helps provide a good foundation for focus in our work. In fact, good nutrition, exercise and rest are necessary for good focus to be possible. Inadequacy in any domain creates noise that makes the practice and engagement of focus far more difficult than it needs to be.

The virtues of multitasking

There are many kinds of work, starting with cooking complex meals, that require the impeccable timing of multiple concurrent tasks. Our success depends on starting and completing several different things at the right times. Multitasking in these contexts is not only not bad, it is not optional. Time management is timing management.

Multitasking is agile fulfillment of multidimensional intentions. It is the opposite of the unfocused distraction and reaction to shiny objects that serve no constellation of intentions.

The more focused we are, the easier and more skillfully we multitask our way to good results. Trying to multitask is a hot mess when we're not focused.

Those of us who regularly observe and work with good multitaskers are struck by the palpable sense of clarity and calmness that emanates from the flow of focus they bring to their work. We don't lose focus because we take on too many things, but because we bring a distracted and reactive mind to complex spaces.

Anywhere, anytime

Anywhere we can imagine being is a perfect venue for the practice of focus.

We can practice waiting for a meeting, in meetings and following up from meetings. We can practice in serendipitous conversations, commuting, traveling and visiting. We can practice doing any kind of research, creativity and collaboration. We can practice in the most mundane tasks and unplugging to refresh.

There is always change to notice at some level of our experience and world. This is how focus contrasts with other practices aimed at creating a clear, calm mind. Focus doesn't require retreating from the world.

Focus connects us more deeply with life outside and inside us. We become more whole, balanced and centered. Everything we experience can be a perfect venue for practice.

Deepening Focus

Consciousness

Ellen Langer talks about focus as mindfulness. She studies mindfulness as noticing what's new in our experience and world. Her research indicates that mindfulness causes us to be creative, agile, passionate, productive, engaged and healthy.

She contrasts it with being mindless. Mindless working is being on automatic, going though the motions, being largely unaware of what's changing, shifting and new within and outside us. Mindlessness is the essence of being distracted and reactive, even in moments when we think we're being very analytical, critical and intellectual.

Being mindless is being conscious, in limited ways. Declaring our status as "the same old same old" is not just words. It accurately describes our unfocused consciousness. Being mindfully focused is a larger consciousness because we're paying attention to how things come together. We notice how change happens. We're focused.

We're beginning to understand consciousness as energy vibration. Each different kind of consciousness we experience in our work and life is a different vibration. The more clear and calm our mind, the more we can feel the vibratory difference between being focused and being unfocused.

Focus shifts our consciousness to a lighter level of energy. That's why we feel like we have so much energy when we're focused.

The joy of focus

In any organization, every individual works and lives somewhere along a continuum from having more moments of feeling happy to more moments of feeling distressed.

In the global study I did for "The Joy of Thriving" I was interested in the question of whether there were any patterns in what made the happiest people happy. I found that by a large margin, they found their greatest joy in discovering new people, places and things.

Serendipitously, I discovered studies on depression looking at the core to people's moments of feeling depressed. Researchers find a lack of attention to novelty in their world.

Dacher Keltner, is psychology researcher and faculty director at UC Berkeley. His study on the impact of emotions relative to inflammation levels indicates the positive emotions reduce inflammations related to all manner of diseases and compromises to wellbeing.

Further studies show that not all positive emotions are equal. There is one that exceeds all others in health and wellbeing: the experience of awe. Awe is the essence of focus, the core to wellbeing.

Shiny Objects

Working without focus doesn't mean working without consciousness. When we are unfocused, our mind is continuously busy in attention to all kinds of shiny objects.

In a world of shiny objects, we pay attention to everything that pops up in conversations and on screens. Each new shiny object leads to next layers of distractions and reactions.

When we're unfocused, everything that demands our attention feels urgent. Everything urgent feels important. We get overwhelmed. We feel stuck between the rocks of urgencies and the hard places of important. The idea of prioritizing things always sounds good until we rediscover the technical impossibility of it because no one in our world considers themselves as less important than everyone else.

The more unfocused we are, the more addicted we become to shiny objects in the form of drama. Until we get focused, our only seeming escape from this addiction are new forms of distraction.

Only when we return to the clear, calm mind of focus do we feel confident in how we decide to use our time.

Unfocused together

Not always knowingly or intentionally, we are complicit co-conspirators in lack of focus.

We distract each other with shiny objects that only serve to reinforce beliefs that some things are *same as always and probably won't change*. We distract each other from noticing changes in our experience and world by recycling the same stories, grievances and commentaries.

We make status updates about static facts. We fill volumes of emails and meetings with mountains of static facts that give us little to no new insights about what's shifting and changing, emerging and transitioning in our world.

We can notice how when we describe our intentions in positive terms of what we want to see, we are more focused together than when we instead create the heavy negative energy of stating intentions in the negative of what we fear and hate.

We design meetings and projects with permeable agenda and participation boundaries that include rich landscapes of new learning and perspectives on what's beyond the walls of our defensive certainties.

When our conversations are about appreciation for change, we become more focused together. With more focus together, we are smarter and faster together.

The wisdom of "don't know"

Studies continue to indicate that one of the top qualities of effective leaders is humility.

At the heart of humility is permission to not know. With the half life of expert knowledge today measured in months rather than years or decades, this humility seems more realistic and wise.

In this world of unprecedented complexity, connectivity and change, we are smarter together. No one of us is smarter than all of us. At the top of organizational risks are people who think they need to or can "know it all." Those of us who have studied the top experts in the world know they measure their value by their questions. It's their questions that most starkly distinguish them from non-experts.

The celebrated psychiatrist and writer R.D. Laing observed that when we don't know we don't know, we think we know.

This is why questions need to precede presentations rather than just follow them. This is why we need to value people for their ability to have good questions more than their ability to have good answers. When we give ourselves and each other permission to not know, we create a more focused organization.

Growth mindsets

Stanford psychologist Carol Dweck talks about fixed and growth mindsets. People who do and feel well at work practice growth mindsets. They believe that the qualities they admire and aspire to can be learned and attained.

People who do not do and feel well at work practice fixed mindsets. They work from a belief that who they think they are cannot be changed. Beliefs have the power to trump the possibilities of neuroplasticity.

Being focused and having a growth mindset are reciprocally related. The more we grow in one dimension, the more we grow in the other. It makes sense that the more we realize change, the more capable of it we think we are.

Windows on the world

Our view of change in our world is as large as the windows we create for it. Our greatest windows on the world are trusted in our expert and collaboration networks. They connect us to all manner of resources that keep us in sync with what is shifting, changing and emerging.

Each publication subscription keeps us in touch with any kind of topic, question and theme possible. These include magazines, newspapers, blogs, conference documents, books and reviews. We keep up with changes in culture and politics, business and technology, psychology and wellbeing.

Whether you've watched a few or hundreds of TED talks, you take away the same awareness that on any given day, there is a universe of interesting and positive changes awaiting our willingness to be focused in our world.

We can grow our local and virtual networks of people with whom we trade on our radars of what's new, shifting and changing. Every serendipitous conversation we invite and accept is a rich possibility space for becoming more focused. Each expands and deepens our capacity for clarity and calmness.

Our sense of focus expands with each connection we make and cultivate with people with differences: different geographies, interests, backgrounds, disciplines, industries and dreams. The more different people are from us, the more focused we become because they are most likely people to open our perspective to change. That's why so many of us feel uniquely focused when we travel.

When we stumble on someone who lives and works with a vibrant sense of focus, they can become for us priceless windows on the world.

The paradoxes of being focused and unfocused

The less we pay attention to change in our experience and world, the more negative energy we feel about change. The more intolerance we have for change, the more unfocused we become. It's a vicious spiral.

Paying attention to change creates a virtuous spiral of focus. Focus makes us more energized than frustrated by the uncertainties implicit in change.

The paradox of being unfocused is that feeling stressed about change, manifested as our intolerance of uncertainty, is actually a function of not paying attention to how things are changing.

As much as we would loudly protest otherwise, we get stressed to the extent we don't notice change, not to the extent that change happens. This explains how people can have completely different reactions to the same changes. Focus makes the difference.

When we become more focused, even about our stress, we discover that all we are doing is replaying the same experience over and over. We're stuck in paradoxical loops of paying attention to how what's changed isn't changing. This keeps us distracted and reactive enough to cease noticing the ubiquity of change from one moment and day to the next.

When we return to being focused, we return to clarity and calmness, which makes us more likely to notice change, feeding an upward virtuous spiral of doing and feeling our best.

Possibility space

Just beyond the horizons of distraction, there is an infinite space of possibilities. When a new perspective, question or idea emerges into our awareness, seemingly from nowhere, it comes from this space. Clarity and calmness open up our access to this space.

Every new challenge, issue and decision in our work requires new possibilities. Before we had creativity research, we superstitiously assumed that creativity was an inherent trait present or missing in different people.

The reality is 90% of us are measurably creative when younger and 90% of us lose this as we get older.

We tend to be more in tune with change when we're younger. Over time, we can grow to give more attention and priority to predictabilities and continuities.

Creativity is a function of focus. As we regain our capacity for focus, we become more creative. We enter any new space of change with optimism and confidence because we feel supported by focused access to the infinite space of possibilities.

The tyranny of lists

It's fascinating, our penchant for lists, our superstitious belief in their power. We daily forgive ourselves, more or less, for not getting our lists right and not getting everything done on our lists.

No matter how diligently and anxiously we engineer and jealousy protect our lists, life happens. Things we cannot predict emerge with promises of equal or more value than the promises of earlier predictive assumptions.

The core mythos underneath our contempt for chaos and lust for an orderly, predictable universe is that focus is about time management and time management is list management. When we understand focus, we realize our best use of time is less about managing lists and more about managing attention.

Lists are assumptions, and as such can make us less focused when we confuse them for the ever-dynamic nature of reality. Lists are maps for the territory. When we're focused, we never confuse map for territory. When our maps differ from territory, we follow the territory.

That is the consciousness, the ever-realistic nature of focus. As we go into any meeting or day, week or quarter with lists of clear intentions of what we will do, we give more energy to the question of what we should give attention to. As a regular practice, this simple, powerful question of where we should put our attention gets and keeps us focused.

When we're focused in our work, our sense of best time use flows from our best attention use.

Uniqueness

Representing centuries old Japanese Zen practices, one of my oldest teachers, Koshin Ogui and his teacher Gyomay Kubose talk about the importance of appreciating uniqueness.

This is seeing the uniqueness of each person and aspect of life. It's realizing no two things are exactly the same. Focus makes this realization possible.

When we appreciate uniqueness, we recognize that differences exist within similarities. We cease using comparisons to divide the world into judgements of better and worse. Older is not worse than younger; younger is not better than older. They are in their own ways different, and uniquely valuable.

Another one my favorite Zen teachers is the New York City social entrepreneur Bernie Glassman who in his book, *Instructions To The Cook*, points out that in the kitchen there are no bad ingredients. Each ingredient is good at different times.

Appreciating uniqueness means realizing the contextual value of everything. This is the basis for wisely affirming the value of polarities as gifts to be engaged at the right time rather than as problems to be eliminated or fixed. This is the power of *and* over the tyranny of *or*.

There are right times to be efficient and generous, centralized and decentralized, critical and promoting, reflective and visionary, waiting and acting, masculine and feminine, internally and externally focused. Each polarity has unique value. Timing is everything.

Urban walks

In her book *On Looking*, Alexandra Horowitz talks about the sensory magnificence of taking the same urban walk with experts from different disciplines like sociology, audiology, medicine, geology and the arts. Our focus is sharpened when our attention to change makes the familiar unfamiliar and the old new.

It's an interesting practice. Take an area of urban blocks and walk through them several different ways on separate occasions. Journal your findings. Here are eight variations to consider noticing.

- The life and evidence of animals and insects
- The array of smells in the air
- The varieties of plants and trees
- Anything in a state of disrepair, decline or decay
- The sounds of traffic, people, birds and other audio events
- Evidence of historical eras, events and influences

- Memories and emotions that emerge in the experience of place
- The variety of physical sensations on the walk

There is another benefit to walking with focus. Stanford studies indicate that we are 80% more creative while walking than sitting. Add that to the recent evidence that sitting is now a top cause of unhealthy living.

Flow

One of the prime influences of my late 1970s graduate studies in positive psychology was the researcher and innovator Mihaly Czikszentmihalyi. He talks about flow.

Flow experiences are those times when we feel completely lost in what we're doing. Our sense of self alters where we feel one with our task and circumstances. In fact, as with all deep experiences of focus, our brain's sense of self-consciousness temporarily diminishes.

In flow, we become 200% faster and 500% more productive in our performance and decision making.

Flow happens naturally and intentionally in just about any kind of situation imaginable. We can experience it in uniquely challenging and routine situations. We can be in flow talking to a group or cooking a meal, in front of a screen or on a walk, playing with ideas or pitching proposals.

Focus is at the core of flow. We lose a separate sense of time and self. We feel completely engaged in what we're doing with the whole of our mind, body and spirit. We live in a rich space of curiosity instead of bouncing back and forth between the poles of stress and boredom.

Focus energizes our experience with curiosity. The more we practice with focus, the more we discover that literally any kind of activity, even waiting, can be a flow activity.

Nature

Nature is magical. It has a unique way of drawing us into focus. With each step, we enter more deeply into sharp clarity and easy calmness.

Contrasted to our many built environments designed for continuities rather than change, nature only offers change. Everything in nature manifests change on a variety of scales in space and time. As focus is about noticing change, nature is an optimal context for this experience.

Nature is the experience of terrains and geological features. It's the feast of attention to a universe of living organisms in various states of development and decay. It's the look, sound, feel and smell of weather and seasons, lightness and darkness. It's the sensual and mythic dimensions of nature evoking focus in our senses and sense making.

For most of us, nature even in small doses, which depending on our dispositions can mean a few hours or days, makes focus most easily possible.

Even when we have available only a few different nature venues, we can optimize our focus practice by varying the timing of our visits. We can visit in different seasons, types of weather, times of day. Taking people or pets who haven't been there before naturally opens our experience to new things revealed through the lens of their fresh experience.

Focus at work

Engagement

The Gallup global research continues to indicate around 70% of employees worldwide are disengaged in their work. Exacerbating the trend is that 80% of their bosses don't even measure for engagement or its root cause, focus. The numbers aren't changing.

One thing people with dominant moments of disengagement have in common across industries and geographies is they work without focus.

The analogy is about a long boat with seven people where two are rowing, two are trying to figure out ways to sink the boat and three others are watching the rowers and complaining about the saboteurs.

People who spend most of their time focused are engaged. They embrace change as it happens in their world and as a result work with a passion to make positive change happen. They row.

People who spend many moments a day unfocused are disengaged. They see every change in their work as more work and do what they can to resist it. Being unfocused drains their emotional energy, giving them a persistent feeling of not having the energy it takes to be resilient to change. Even when they are compensated for supposedly taking on more, any more beyond that is easy cause for resistance.

Many people whose habit is being unfocused can learn to be more focused in their work. There is something about them that longs for clarity and calmness, and they have no idea how to develop these in their work. They have no idea focus is an option until they learn that and how it is.

People who work with them can have an important influence on the possibility of this learning.

It takes the simple practice of including them in any conversations about any kind of change in their world. It's being curious about any kinds of changes that might be happening for them in their experience, their work and their world.

Focus is contagious. The more people practice and talk about their focus, the more contagious their energy is. When five of seven people row, quite often the two who don't feel like they belong step up or step out.

There is no pressure in human experience like peer pressure. No amount of accountability and incentive programs can come close to the power of peer influence.

Meetings

In the conversations we call meetings, we show up collectively more focused or unfocused.

In unfocused meetings, people endlessly discuss and argue over what they already know in recycled monologues. New information is dismissed or treated with suspicion. The group divides into talkers and listeners. As people feel unheard, they become more unfocused together.

In focused meetings, the energy is alive with curiosity and insights into what's shifting and changing for the group and its world. New information is invited and valued, people feel heard and the group becomes more focused together.

This explains the success of the simple, powerful collaboration model, The Agile Canvas. We're continuously asking new questions, making new discoveries. We're updating and adapting everything to the constant of change. The process keeps people continuously focused, realistic and productive.

When we work with focus, status meetings aren't static meetings. They don't ask just for data points of what's happened or is happening. We ask for what's changing, what's different in this two week sprint than the last, what's shifting in the rhythms of time.

When it's a decision or idea meeting, we ask about what's new for ourselves and our world. When we are in sync with change, it's interesting how we tend to do the right things at the right times.

The feedback conundrum

Feedback appears in myriad forms. There is the feedback we share and exchange in conversations, emails and texts, performance reviews, project and event critiques, town hall meetings, surveys and focus groups.

Feedback can support or prevent focus. We have feedback no one has asked for. People have feedback for us they're giving us not at all or not in useful ways. In organizational cultures that have not kept up with the latest science on personal and collective growth, feedback features more emphasis on weaknesses and failures than strengths and successes.

As it turns out from hundreds of studies, our weaknesses are not responsible for moments of focus and doing our best. Our greatest growth potentials are in the areas of our strengths.

When we are focused, our relationship to feedback is characterized by clarity and calmness. We give and receive useful feedback. It is not an opportunity for distraction from our goodness and the goodness of others.

When we are focused and we ask for, offer and share feedback with someone, we talk about how things are changing for both of us. We express curiosity about why things are shifting as they are.

We expect change. We don't assume the kinds of feedback we gave people before would be useful to them now. We ask for what would be useful for us now. We don't assume the kinds of feedback we found useful once are kinds that would be useful today.

Only when we experience the clarity and calmness of focus are we capable of inviting, sharing and using useful feedback.

Oh, the buttons they push

When it comes to our capacity for being reactive, we work with two kinds of people. There are those who knowingly push our buttons and those who unknowingly push our buttons.

Either way, we can lose focus. We can get reactively defensive or offensive. We don't do and feel our best. Until we return to focus, it infects the rest of our work and life.

One of the things our brain is good at doing is making sure every kind of event we have has an emotional tag associated with it. Our brain doesn't care what kind of emotional tags it gives events.

Anytime we experience a similar event, our brain triggers the associated emotional tag and we automatically feel versions of similar emotions. The triggered emotions distract us from whatever else we might be feeling and giving attention to at the time.

The tags keep working perfectly until we weaken them. We weaken them every time we go into a space of focus when they happen.

When we create a space of focus, we notice how our experience of any reactive emotions changes and shifts from one moment to the next, even in subtle ways. Our neuroplastic brain has no intrinsic attachment to any tags it creates.

By the way

In traditionally designed organizations, a class of thinkers gets to prioritize and mandate work to a class of doers. Thinkers can feel free to be fairly focused or unfocused in their prioritizing and mandating. Most organizations don't even know how to measure for focus.

If you're in the thinking class, being focused means regularly checking in with people, peers and doer class folks, to see what's changing. When you work with focus, you get more done and so does everyone else.

If you're in the doer class, you can punctuate every conversation and email with a "By the way ..." introducing any kinds of change happening that might be relevant to those you engage in them. This creates a sense of positive suspicion. Thinkers grow more suspicious of their assumptions because you're inviting them kindly to suspect things are changing beyond their static assumptions. That's a good day.

Either way, never deny your power by postponing your being focused until others are.

Charts and graphs

Some people thrive on charts and graphs. It's how they measure their worth and assess the value of others. They say the numbers tell the story. Sometimes they do.

Not everything we measure gives us a rich sense of how change is emerging and happening in our world. Not everything measured matters. Many things that matter cannot be measured. If we have enough degrees and certificates, we know how to engineer static charts and graphs that actually obscure more than reveal the patterns and qualities of change. In the worst cases, charts and graphs plot the trends of norms and averages, leaving narratives to reveal outliers representing windows to new possibilities.

When we're focused, we do not assume that any two dimensional picture reveals all the trends, opportunities and possibilities shifting and changing in our world. We pay as much attention to the three dimensionality of narratives that live beyond the edges of even the most carefully detailed charts and graphs.

Anti-ToDo Lists

The famously successful entrepreneur Marc Andreessen stays focused with his anti-todo list. Throughout his day, he adds to his planned todo lists all the done items that didn't appear originally on his planned lists.

The practice keeps us in constant touch with how we and our world change. It gives us space to enjoy each accomplishment rather than daily berate ourselves for all the planned items that went undone.

Teresa Amabile's Harvard happiness studies demonstrate that the most significant source of happiness at work is the simple and frequent recognition of progress and accomplishment.

The practice of anti-todo lists creates the clarity and calmness of this practice.

Sane and crazy

We learn to label people. It's the practice of generalization intrinsic to being unfocused. The field of psychotherapeutic diagnostics continues to invent new labels. Older pre-empirical theories urge us to believe that people in fact are the labels authorized experts confer on them.

Adding to the evidence of neuroplasticity in the brain, the epigenetics research indicates that our chosen behaviors and thought practices influence gene expression in conditions we have associated with genetically based psychological labels.

All of this adds up to the notion that while a lack of focus would argue that people are either sane or crazy, being focused would suggest that everyone has different ratios and tempos of sane and crazy moments.

Focus always notices the changes and shifts in all of us from one day and moment to the next. Focus sees more nuanced textures of human experience because it pays attention to the context of experience where change lives.

This applies to all labels. When we are tempted to label others and ourselves as smart or not smart, introverts or extroverts, risk takers or risk avoiders, focus brings us back to the reality that we all have moments of these, in different proportions.

This is a liberating realization, making both sides of every polarity more available. We become more whole.

When we are more whole we act with more confidence, poise, wisdom and agility. We become more skillful and connected in everything we attempt and do.

Drama

The distractions and reactions of being unfocused are the currencies of drama. They make drama possible.

Drama comes in variety of shapes and sizes. The more we practice focus, the more we realize how drama is self-created, and optional.

There is the drama of deprivation. We invest time and energy dwelling on the many things other people have or that we believe we are entitled to and lack. We tag things we experience in our world as continuous reminders of our deficiencies. We use free time to wound and abuse ourselves with reminders of our deprived and inferior existence.

There is the drama of victimhood. We spend time in memories about and interactions with people intent on controlling us. We wallow in self-pity and a persistent sense of unworthiness, of not measuring up to standards that are unknown, unfulfillable, or both.

We focus on how awful they are and usually get around to punishing ourselves more than they do with repeated narratives of our victimhood.

Focus makes drama less necessary and likely because we make life more interesting than any drama affords.

Everything is our teacher

Focus makes everything our teacher.

When we are unfocused, we feel a sense of tension with things we consider the enemy. We waste time fighting things. We live in a space of negative energy.

When we are focused, our clarity and calmness emerges from a sense that everything is our teacher. Things that would otherwise bother us remind us of our intentions. We transform them into reminders of what matters most to us.

We feel grateful for these reminders and are no longer distracted and reactive. They no longer sap our energy. We are instead energized by returning to the lighter energy vibrations of focus on our intentions.

We regain our power.

Being in control

Each of us has our own uncertainty thresholds. Some of us have little tolerance for uncertainty. We try to plan our world as best we can so it doesn't surprise us unless we want it to. Some of us tolerate uncertainty. Some of us thrive on it.

It's an issue because no organization or industry today is protected from uncertainty. However much we invest in promises of a guaranteed future, the future remains intrinsically unknowable. Change is a constant and resisting change is its own suffering.

The less tolerance we have for uncertainty, the more we feel the need to control ourselves, the people and things in our world. Not everyone appreciates these intentions, no matter how sincere or inspired. Not that many people at work nightly pray to be controlled by others.

People who feel the need to be in control often have long lists of evidentiary achievements and crises averted they attribute specifically, often superstitiously, to their being in control. These accomplishments come at high costs. People have to work overtime to achieve and protect control because the need to be in control makes us more unfocused, more distracted and reactive.

The data has little support for control based organizations, indicating instead that self-organizing, aligned groups of focused and connected people significantly outperform externally controlled groups.

The need to control makes it less likely that people will notice how change happens in themselves and their world because all their attention is given to getting rid of change in order to eliminate intolerable uncertainties.

The more people feel controlled, the more unfocused they become, which causes others to try controlling them more, sending everyone into a vicious spiral of being increasingly unfocused.

People who don't feel the need to control things actually get more done and at less cost because they are focused. Focus is the functional alternative to the precipitous mission of trying to engineer a world where the only change is the one we give permission for.

What futurists do, really

Innovative organizations are always looking for the next new thing that can catapult them into their next trajectories of growth and success.

Many strategically consort with futurists, the people dedicated to knowing what's bubbling up on the horizons of wow.

They don't have a crystal ball into the intrinsically unknowable future any more than anyone else. What they are good at is paying attention to the macro and micro promising innovative, technical, economic, social, cultural and political trends. It also helps that the better futurists have well-honed intuitions.

When we want a more focused sense of the future, we can be our own futuristas.

We have the kinds of probable and improbable conversations and do the kind of diverse research it takes to notice changes few others see. That's what makes innovators innovative.

Quality introductions, quality connections

When we want to connect and reconnect with people, the quality of our connections begins with the quality of our introductions.

The weakest introductions feature exchanges about things not changing in our life, our work and world. These are the seemingly static data points of our title, tenure, residence and birth locations, number and ages of children, personal likes and annoyances. These dominate unfocused introductions.

Rich, focused introductions instead feature discoveries of what's shifting in our respective and overlapping worlds. We talk about our experience and inquire into theirs. We share comparisons between today and yesterday, this and last week, this and last month, this and last year.

When we are focused together, we are connected together. Trust builds. Trust is the dog that wags the tail of culture. It doesn't have to be more complicated that this.

Kindness

One of the signature qualities of strong organizational cultures is a culture of trust. Culture is significant because when it comes to the growth and success potential of any organization, culture trumps strategy and structure. Trust is significant because we move together at the speed of trust.

Intrinsic to a culture of trust is kindness. People trust spaces characterized by kindness.

In our life and work, we are as kind as we are focused. We are not kind when we are unfocused in distraction and reactivity. We tend to be fairly self-centered when we are unfocused, making kindness less possible. We become relatively unhelpful in what we do and say, and what we don't do and don't say.

The clarity and calmness of focus make kindness more possible. With clarity and calmness we are more patient to listen, inquire and share.

We take time for stories because they speak louder than facts and demands. We are more persistent and rigorous. Unless we have immutable evidence that something can't be done, we act with the agile, self-fulfilling belief that it can.

We generously offer and ask for help because both are acts of kindness making things easier for all of us and making it easier for all of us to feel valued for our gifts.

Charles Limb and Allen Braun have research on musical improvisation the National Institutes of Health. Brain scans show that when musicians are improvising as in jazz, they go into a flow state and lose self-consciousness the way we do in acts of kindness.

It's interesting to see the relationships between kindness, empathy and creativity and their implications when we seek innovation and cultures of trust.

Listening

When we listen with focus, we notice shifts and changes in what people are saying and all of their expressive energy providing the media for their messages. We notice the unfolding of their thinking and perspectives.

When we offer questions, we offer them with an intention to discover something new, some new details, feelings or details in their experience. We also notice shifts and changes in our own experience and expressions in the interaction.

Listening has two dimensions, internal and external. Internal listening is our experience of what other people are expressing. It is our sense making of what they offer in the conversation. External listening is how we respond.

There are a handful of common external listening responses.

We affirm the truth and value of what we hear. We ask thoughtful questions that invite new levels of understanding of the other person's experience and world.

We deny the truth and value of what we hear. We deceive with signs of listening, interest or agreeing to appear as if we're listening, interested or agreeing. We deflect by not responding to what we hear and instead go on to talk about something else or to someone else.

Focus makes listening to feel heard more possible. Being unfocused in our listening makes it more possible that we deny, deceive or deflect because we get caught in loops of their thinking or ours.

We do usually not have direct access to each other's internal experience beyond what we make transparent in words and actions. Until we respond externally, people usually can't know if and how we listen to anything they express.

People experience the quality of our internal listening only through the quality of our external listening. When we want people to feel more heard, it's about how we respond with external listening.

Each of the common ways to respond with external listening offers a continuum of possibilities in how heard people feel with us and how heard we feel with them. The more heard we and others feel, the more we show up with focus. The more generous and creative we become together.

The people we care for

We have people who depend on us. They are the people in our work groups, our families and friends, our customers and clients, people who feel responsible for our performance and the people impacted by the intended and unintended consequences of our actions and deliverables. They depend on us helping them succeed.

At any point in time, we are more focused or unfocused in our relationships with them.

When we are unfocused, we fail to be curious about what's different, shifting and changing for them from moment to moment, day to day, month to month, year to year. The more distracted and reactive we are in these relationships, the less clear and calm we are with them.

Observation and curiosity support our noticing how things change for them. We pay attention and inquire with the expectation that change is a constant for them and an intention to discover how things are changing for them.

When we are focused, we spend less time assuming their claim of "same old" has any possible relationship to reality. Their unfocused inattention to change doesn't have to be ours as well. We don't have to take on their lack of focus. In fact, our being focused naturally opens for them the possibility of focus.

When we are unfocused in being distracted and reactive, our time with others who depend on us is always too much time. When we are focused, no matter how much time we have with people who depend on us, it is quality time because we are present with a palpable and often contagious sense of focus.

Leadership as remindership

Most organizations still practice two class systems of power, responsibility and knowledge haves and have-nots. Others are quickly moving to more engaging models of distributed and collaborative power, responsibility and knowledge.

In any context, a leader's work is to remind people to focus through inquiry, modeling and storytelling.

We remind people through the questions we raise in conversations, whatever media of choice. We remind them through the connections we make between them and others. Each story we share can be a reminder.

When we understand that people always do the best they can based on the quality of their attention at the time, we understand that the heart of leadership is remindership.

Focused organizations

It's interesting to read about and visit organizations currently admired for their innovative products and services, brands and cultures.

There's always something different about them. It's not just their rock star founders or leaders. It's the whole way they do business not as usual. We get the impression that they are interested in anything but what worked before.

I would argue that one thing they have in common is focus. They are focused in their markets and their people are focused in their work. Everyone seems to be in the right place at the right time, doing the right things for the right reasons.

We get to do that when we're in sync with change within and around us. We're in sync with change when we work and show up with focus. Few things happen well when we're out of sync with change, when we're unfocused in distraction and reaction.

Think about all the things that can distract you, your group and your organization from noticing change. Think about all the things that can make you, your group and your organization reactive.

These become less relevant with focus. With focus, we enjoy doing well. The more focused we become in our markets, the more our markets focus on us. We can begin exploring how to design focused organizations. It will be a new, amazing world.

Courage

When we work with focus we work with courage.

Courage is the ability to speak our truth, offer our gifts, ask for help and in fact ask for anything we think would make things better for everyone. We are fearless. Our energy is boundless. We live in the infinite vibratory space of possibilities. We are inspired by change, and for change. We connect in change.

Courage energizes us with a sense that anything we can intend as possible becomes more possible. We dare to declare the possibility of impossible, having seen that achieved in countless ways by the most focused people on the planet.

In flawless focus, we work with flawless courage. Our work becomes a rich media for our personal and shared transformation. This is the simple power of focus.

Jack Ricchiuto

Jack Ricchiuto is a writer, teacher and master storyteller. His work is about how we can make a positive difference together in our work and world.

Over the past 3 decades, Jack has worked in over two dozen industry sectors with hundreds of organizations and communities across the US and globally. He is a partner with Ernst & Young, Thrive@Work, The Auorm Group and Learn2Story.

Jack has worked with multi-national companies and non-profits like IBM, PayPal, NASA, American Red Cross, FedEx, Federal Reserve Bank, USDA, Smuckers and investment leaders from Silicon Valley. He has taught in graduate and post-graduate programs at Harvard Kennedy Business School, UC Berkeley, Vanderbilt and teaching Leadership for 15 years in Kent State University's EMBA program.

Jack earned a graduate degree in positive psychology from Goddard College and was trained by global leaders in American, European and Japanese therapeutic transformation models. He was one of the first web site designers, bloggers and social media and network experts.

Jack's books include *Collaborative Creativity, Accidental Conversations, Project Zen, Appreciative Leadership, Mountain Paths, Conscious Becoming, Instructions from the Cook, The Stories that Connect Us, The Enchantment of Casual Origins, The Joy of Thriving, Ordinary Eyes, The Agile Canvas Field Guide, Abundant Possibilities, The Power Of Circles, Making Sense Of Time, Beyond Recipes* and *Focus.*

For more about Jack, his books and work visit JackRicchiuto.com

To order copies and explore workshops and coaching based on the book, visit FocusAtWork.info